I0606020

WNBA Hot Ticket

INDIANA FEVER

JOSH ANDERSON

Lerner Publications ◆ Minneapolis

To Leo and Dane, the biggest superstars I've ever met.

The stats and information in this book are accurate through July 2024.

Copyright © 2025 by Lerner Publishing Group, Inc.

All rights reserved. International copyright secured. No part of this book may be reproduced, stored in a retrieval system, or transmitted in any form or by any means—electronic, mechanical, photocopying, recording, or otherwise—without the prior written permission of Lerner Publishing Group, Inc., except for the inclusion of brief quotations in an acknowledged review.

Lerner Publications Company
An imprint of Lerner Publishing Group, Inc.
241 First Avenue North
Minneapolis, MN 55401 USA

For reading levels and more information, look up this title at www.lernerbooks.com.

Main body text set in Aptifer Slab LT Pro / Typeface provided by Linotype AG

Library of Congress Cataloging-in-Publication Data

Names: Anderson, Josh, author.
Title: Indiana Fever / Josh Anderson.
Description: Minneapolis, MN : Lerner Publications, 2025. | Series: Lerner sports. WNBA hot ticket | Includes bibliographical references and index. | Audience: Ages 7–11 | Audience: Grades 2–3 | Summary: "The Indiana Fever won the 2012 WNBA Championship, but they haven't had much success lately. Meet the team's players, coaches, and fans, and find out why Cailin Clark is bringing renewed hope to the team"— Provided by publisher.
Identifiers: LCCN 2024026069 (print) | LCCN 2024026070 (ebook) | ISBN 9798765669709 (library binding) | ISBN 9798765669914 (paperback) | ISBN 9798765669938 (epub)
Subjects: LCSH: Indiana Fever (Basketball team)—Juvenile literature.
Classification: LCC GV885.52.I525 A64 2025 (print) | LCC GV885.52.I525 (ebook) | DDC 796.323/6409772—dc23/eng/20240613

TABLE OF CONTENTS

Caitlin Clark scored 3,951 points during her four years at the University of Iowa.

A BUDDING SUPERSTAR

FACTS AT A GLANCE

- **TAMIKA CATCHINGS**, who played her entire career for the fever, leads the Women's National Basketball Association (WNBA) in career steals. She ranks third all-time in points.
- The Fever had the first overall pick in the WNBA Draft in 2023 and 2024. They used those picks on **ALIYAH BOSTON** and **CAITLIN CLARK**.
- The Fever's first playoff series win was in 2005 against the **NEW YORK LIBERTY**.
- From 2009 to 2015, the Indiana Fever played in three **WNBA FINALS** and won the team's only title in 2012.

Caitlin Clark's first game as a pro basketball player didn't start as she had hoped it would. Early in the Indiana Fever's 2024 season opener against the Connecticut Sun, Clark dribbled toward the basket and attempted a layup. It was a shot she'd hit thousands of times in her life. But the ball hit the backboard and missed the rim. Then she missed her next two shots. To make matters worse, she also committed two fouls and a turnover in the first quarter.

Never before had the world been so excited to see a WNBA rookie play in her first game. As college basketball's all-time leading scorer, Clark had brought countless new fans to women's basketball. She was often compared to National Basketball Association (NBA) legend Stephen Curry of the Golden State Warriors. Thanks to Clark's presence on the visiting team, the Connecticut Sun had their first season-opener sellout since 2003.

Clark and everyone watching knew that her first moments on a WNBA court had not shown what she could do. She finally sank her first shot about halfway through the second quarter. Even though she finished the game with plenty to improve upon, Clark had 20 points in the game. It was more than any other player on her team scored that night in the Fever's 92–71 loss.

Since their last playoff appearance in 2016, the Fever have been one of the worst teams in the WNBA. But with the game's most popular player on their roster, the basketball world has its eyes on Indiana. Fans want to see if they can compete for their second WNBA title.

Clark attempted 15 shots during her first WNBA game. She made five of them.

Clark dribbles around the Sun's DiJonai Carrington in the Fever's first game of the 2024 season.

Alicia Thompson attempts to score for the Fever in a 2000 game against the Seattle Storm.

The Indiana Fever began as an expansion team during the WNBA's fourth season in 2000. That year, the league added four teams and grew to 16 overall. In 2024, the league had 12 teams. The Fever's arena, Gainbridge Fieldhouse, opened in 1999. The Fever have played all of their home games there.

The Fever share Gainbridge Fieldhouse with the NBA's Indiana Pacers. The teams are both owned by businessperson Herb Simon.

Gainbridge Fieldhouse seats 20,000 basketball fans for Fever and Pacers games.

The Fever's name comes from Indiana's long history with basketball. Indianans love hoops so much that they have a fever for the sport.

During their first season, the Fever were coached by women's basketball legend Anne Donovan. Donovan is a member of the Women's Basketball Hall of Fame. She won a college national championship and two Olympic gold medals as a player. Despite Donovan's successful playing history, Indiana was one of the worst teams in the league during their first two seasons.

Then, in 2002, a rookie named Tamika Catchings changed everything. Catchings led the Fever to their first playoff appearance in 2002. The future Hall of Fame player brought Indiana to 12 playoff

Anne Donovan went on to coach four other WNBA teams after coaching Indiana.

Tamika Catchings shoots over two Phoenix Mercury defenders during the 2009 WNBA Finals.

appearances in a row from 2005 to 2016. It was during this amazing playoff streak that the Fever won their only WNBA title in 2012.

Since their last playoff appearance in 2016, the Fever have struggled on the court. The team's lowest point came from 2020 to 2022 when Indiana won only 17 games over three seasons. Their 5–31 record in 2022 was the worst in team history.

HOOPS SCOOP

More than two million people watched the Fever choose Caitlin Clark in the 2024 WNBA Draft.

WNBA commissioner Cathy Engelbert (*right*) presents Caitlin Clark with a Fever jersey during the 2024 Draft.

In most pro sports, the teams with the poorest records get to pick ahead of the other teams in the draft. This gives the losing teams a strong chance to improve. The Fever's losing records in 2022 and 2023 allowed them to pick first overall in both the 2023 and 2024 WNBA Drafts. The Fever added Aliyah Boston and Caitlin Clark with those picks. Fans hope their new superstar players mean a much brighter future is just around the corner.

BECOMING ADVOCATES

In addition to the team's efforts to succeed on the court, Fever players and staff are leaders in their communities as well. Partnering with Indiana University and Anthem, Inc., the Fever started the Athlete to Advocate program. Over five weeks, players learned how to use their voices to help address social injustice and help communities that need it. Many players found it a positive experience and a building block to become true advocates for change.

Programs such as Athlete to Advocate give players a chance to make a difference off the court.

Tamika Catchings averaged 16.1 points per game during her 15 years with the Fever.

FEVER GREATS

No player in Fever history has done more on the court than Tamika Catchings. She joined Indiana in 2002 and spent her entire 15-season WNBA career with the Fever. Catchings was chosen for 10 WNBA All-Star Games and led the team to the playoffs 13 times. She won the WNBA Most Valuable Player (MVP) award in 2011. Then, in 2012, Catchings led Indiana to its only championship. She won the WNBA Finals MVP award.

Catchings is the league's all-time leader in steals. She ranks third in points and fifth in rebounds. Catchings also won four Olympic gold medals playing for the USA Basketball Women's National Team. After retiring as a player, Catchings worked for the Fever in a variety of important jobs. She was the team's general manager from 2017 to 2022.

The USA Basketball Women's National Team celebrates their gold medal win at the 2016 Olympics.

Catchings's former coach, Lin Dunn, took over the position of general manager when Catchings left the Fever. Dunn coached the Fever for seven seasons from 2008 to 2014. She led the Fever to the Finals twice and was the team's coach when they won the 2012 WNBA title.

One of Dunn's top players was Katie Douglas. The five-time All-Star played for the Fever from 2008 to 2013. She ranks third in team history in scoring. Douglas averaged 17.7 points in the 2012 Eastern Conference Finals against the Connecticut Sun.

Lin Dunn (*left*) became the general manager of the Indiana Fever in 2022.

One of the Fever's current players, Kelsey Mitchell, already ranks second all-time in scoring for Indiana. Mitchell has ranked in the top 10 in three-point baskets made every season of her career. She's been a top-10 scorer four times and received her first All-Star selection in 2023.

After winning a national championship and the college Player of the Year award in 2022 with the University of South Carolina, Aliyah Boston was picked first overall by the Fever in the 2023 WNBA Draft. As a rookie, Boston led the Fever in blocks and steals, averaging 14.5 points and 8.4 rebounds per game. She was named Rookie of the Year and was picked for the All-Star team.

The Fever picked point guard Kelsey Mitchell second overall in the 2018 WNBA Draft.

Caitlin Clark has already made a huge impact on the game. Nearly 19 million people watched Clark's final college game, the 2024 college national championship, on television. Clark's University of Iowa team lost to South Carolina. For the first time, more people watched the women's final than the men's final. Some WNBA teams have moved their games against the Fever into larger arenas to meet the huge demand for tickets.

Early in her first season, Clark set a new record. She became the first rookie in WNBA history to score 30 points in a game while also logging five rebounds, five assists, three blocked shots, and three steals. While it's too early to know if Clark will become one of the league's greatest players, many people expect she will.

Caitlin Clark shoots over the New York Liberty's Ivana Dojkić in a 2024 game.

HOOPS SCOOP

In 2023, Aliyah Boston (*right*) became the second Fever player in team history to win the WNBA's Rookie of the Year award.

Guard Shavonte Zellous celebrates the Fever's WNBA championship win in 2012.

CHAMPIONS

The Fever were locked in a tight contest in Game 4 of the 2012 WNBA Finals against the Minnesota Lynx. Indiana led most of the way, but the Lynx wouldn't back down. The Fever's first WNBA title was at stake.

The Lynx scored to pull within three points, 68–65. Only about seven minutes remained on the game clock. Guarded by the Lynx's best player, future WNBA MVP Maya Moore, Fever star Tamika Catchings dribbled the ball up the court.

Tamika Catchings (*left*) and Erlana Larkins (*right*) try to keep Monica Wright from scoring for the Minnesota Lynx during the 2012 WNBA Finals.

Catchings dribbled around Moore. Another Lynx defender stepped up. But Catchings soared over her for a layup. The ball hit the backboard and dropped into the basket. The shot gave Catchings two of her 25 points in the game and helped propel the Fever to an 87–78 victory. The 2012 WNBA title was the first and only for Indiana in team history.

The quest for that title had begun 12 years earlier on June 1, 2000. That day, the Fever played their first WNBA game. It took place in Florida against the Miami Sol. Alicia Thompson scored 13 points to lead the Fever to an exciting 57–54 victory.

Fever players celebrate their WNBA championship win with team owner Herb Simon (*center*).

Forward Kelly Schumacher shoots the ball. She played for the Fever from 2001 to 2005.

The Fever's first taste of playoff success came in 2005. Indiana swept their first-round series against the New York Liberty before losing in the Eastern Conference Finals. The 2005 season was the first of 12 straight playoff appearances for Catchings and the Fever.

HOOPS SCOOP

Tamika Catchings is the WNBA's all-time leader in playoff points, rebounds, and steals.

Tamika Catchings (*center*) scored 61 points during the 2015 Finals.

Indiana nearly captured its first title in 2009 when it played in the Finals against the Phoenix Mercury and that season's WNBA MVP, Diana Taurasi. The Fever lost in Game 1, falling 120–116 in overtime. Indiana won the next two games to get one win away from the title. But the Mercury won Games 4 and 5, so fans in Indiana would have to wait for a championship.

After winning the WNBA title in 2012, the Fever made the Finals again in 2015. It was a rematch with the Lynx, the team Indiana defeated in the 2012 Finals. This time, after the Fever won Game 1 in Minnesota, the Lynx won three of the next four games. Indiana fell short of a second championship in an exciting five-game series.

Katie Douglas (*right*) played six seasons with the Fever from 2008 to 2013.

Early in her first WNBA season, Caitlin Clark led the league in three-point attempts.

CHAPTER 4

A BRIGHT FUTURE

The WNBA and women's hoops are on the rise. Some of the fan excitement is due to Caitlin Clark, but she is only one of many exciting and talented players in the league. After shrinking from a high of 16 teams in the early 2000s down to 12, the league will expand for the first time in more than a decade in 2025. The Valkyries will play in Northern California in the same arena as the NBA's Golden State Warriors. Another team will begin play in Toronto, Canada, in 2026.

The Fever have had one of the league's worst records in recent years, but there is so much hope and excitement for the team and its young star players. Even though the Fever were near the bottom of the standings in 2023, the team sent two players, Kelsey Mitchell and

Aliyah Boston (*center*) pumps up her teammates before a 2024 game.

Aliyah Boston, to the WNBA All-Star Game. Winning the draft lottery in 2023 allowed Indiana to add Clark to their roster.

From 2009 to 2015, the Fever played in three WNBA Finals and won the team's only WNBA title. But since 2016, the team has missed the playoffs every season. Sports fans in Indiana love basketball, and they hope Clark can team up with Boston, Mitchell, and their other talented teammates to lead the Fever back to the playoffs and the Finals.

Kelsey Mitchell (*left*) and Aliyah Boston (*right*) work to keep Myisha Hines-Allen of the Washington Mystics from grabbing a rebound.

In her first six seasons on the team, Kelsey Mitchell (*right*) scored 3,156 points for the Fever.

GLOSSARY

advocate: a person who argues for, recommends, or supports a cause

All-Star: a player chosen as one of the best in the league to compete in a game against other top players

draft: when teams take turns choosing new players

draft lottery: an event to determine the order for a draft. In the WNBA, teams that missed the playoffs the year before take part in the lottery.

expansion team: a team added to an existing sports league

hoops: basketball

layup: a shot in basketball made from near the basket, usually by playing the ball off the backboard

rebound: grabbing and controlling the ball after a missed shot

rookie: a first-year player

roster: a list of players on a team

steal: when a basketball player takes the ball from an opposing player

turnover: losing the ball to the opposing team

LEARN MORE

Caitlin Clark
https://caitlinclark22.com/

Hanlon, Luke. *Caitlin Clark: Basketball Star.* Minneapolis: Abdo, 2025.

Indiana Fever
https://fever.wnba.com/

Leed, Percy. *Pro Basketball by the Numbers*. Minneapolis: Lerner Publications, 2025.

Whiting, Jim. *The Story of the Indiana Fever.* Mankato, Minnesota: Creative Education and Creative Paperbacks, 2024.

WNBA
https://www.wnba.com/

INDEX

PHOTO ACKNOWLEDGMENTS

Image credits: Elsa/Getty Images Sport/Getty Images, p.4; Elsa/Getty Images Sport/Getty Images, p.6; M. Anthony Nesmith/Icon Sportswire/Getty Images, p.7; Otto Greule Jr./Allsport/Getty Images, p.8; Dylan Buell/Getty Images Sport/Getty Images, p.9; Otto Greule Jr./Allsport/Getty Images, p.10; Andy Lyons/Getty Images Sport/Getty Images, p.11; Sarah Stier/Getty Images Sport/Getty Images, p.12; Todd Warshaw/Allsport/Getty Images, p.13; Michael Hickey/Getty Images Sport/Getty Images, p.14; Tim Clayton/Corbis/Getty Images, p.15; Andy Lyons/Getty Images Sport/Getty Images, p.16; Sarah Stier/Getty Images Sport/Getty Images, p.17; Elsa/Getty Images Sport/Getty Images, p.18; Sarah Stier/Getty Images Sport/Getty Images, p.19; Michael Hickey/Getty Images Sport/Getty Images, p.20; Michael Hickey/Getty Images Sport/Getty Images, p.21; Michael Hickey/Getty Images Sport/Getty Images, p.22; Karl Crutchfield/Ai Wire/Newscom, p.23; Andy Lyons/Getty Images Sport/Getty Images, p.24; Christian Petersen/Getty Images Sport/Getty Images, p.25; Emilee Chinn/Getty Images Sport/Getty Images, p.26; Steph Chambers/Getty Images Sport/Getty Images, p.27; G Fiume/Getty Images Sport/Getty Images, p.28; G Fiume/Getty Images Sport/Getty Images, p.29

Cover image: M. Anthony Nesmith/Icon Sportswire/Getty Images